Jon's Heart

Jon's Heart

Jon Waldrop

Ty and the Knight Writer LLC

CONTENTS

1. DREAMT OF YOU ... 1
2. NEVER SEEN SUCH ... 2
3. THINKING ABOUT YOU ... 3
4. YOU ARE ... 4
5. EVEN IN MY DREAMS ... 5
6. YOU ARE ... 6
7. ANOTHER DAY ... 7
8. FINALLY, OVER ... 8
9. SITTING THERE ... 9
10. EVERY TIME I SEE ... 10
11. ANOTHER DAY ... 11
12. NEVER FELT THIS ... 12
13. NEVER GONE SO ... 13

CONTENTS

14	ANOTHER LONELY DAY	14
15	DISTANCE	15
16	BEST OF MY DAYS	16
17	LOVE POEM FOR CRUSH	17
18	SO MUCH TO SAY	18
19	NEED TO SEE YOUR FACE	19
20	MOMENTS	20
21	YOU	21
22	ALONE WITHOUT YOU	22
23	EMERGED	23
24	HEARTBREAK	24
25	TIME OF DAY	25
26	OPEN UP	26
27	COLDNESS	27
28	TELLING YOU HOW	28
29	WHERE I WANT TO BE	29
30	MOMENT OF MEETING	30

CONTENTS

31 | EVERY TIME YOU 31

32 | EXCITED 32

33 | FOR THE DAY 33

34 | SUNNY DAY'S 34

35 | IN THE END 35

1

DREAMT OF YOU

Dreamt of you last night, the thought
        Was such a delight, had been so long
        The dream at first felt wrong. Do i
     Have the right to see your face, regardless
       Of the fight, having you talk to me felt
       So very right.

NEVER SEEN SUCH

Never seen such Beauty in my life
You are such a sight, it would
Take all my might to stay away.
The feelings I have make me feel
like I can fly
Needing you close, the dreams
I have are not enough
Being without you is beyond rough.

THINKING ABOUT YOU

Been thinking about you all day long
    But the feelings make me feel like I am wrong
Need to see your face because it makes me smile
    It keeps me going through all the miles
    I know I should not feel this way
    But all I do as I lay here is think if you.
      Never seen such a beauty in my
    Life, being without you would
  Cause me such strife.

YOU ARE

Being swept up in your eyes
    Hoping them never tell me lies
        Hearing your voice gives me Goosebumps
            And a lump in my throat
        Please don't leave me, I would
    Never be able to feel again this free.

EVEN IN MY DREAMS

Even in my dreams I see your face
      My Mind races with thoughts, of you and
   Me, the need spreads through me like a wave
          Of Grief.

YOU ARE

Being swept up in your eyes
 Hoping them never tell me lies
 Hearing your voice gives me Goosebumps
 And a lump in my throat
 Please don't leave me, I would
 Never be able to feel again this free.

ANOTHER DAY

Another day another lost
      What did it cost? Finding my way
     Through the dark, all my cries seem to
    Fall off the mark. Crying and Crying
   Yet no one to hear, left alone
     To dissolve in fear.

FINALLY, OVER

Among the darkness and blind trust
    My feelings for you have turned to rust
   Never to return, but I have learned
So much, needing you has subsided
    The feeling of wanting your touch
      I figured out were just plain lies.
  Now I move on knowing that
Everything I felt and thought has died.

9

SITTING THERE

Seeing you sitting there makes me feel so bear
    To be able to speak to you would be a dream
      come true. Your brown hair looks so
        Would it be rude to tell you that you
    look so good?
     Rarely have I felt this need,
    The feelings that I have make
   me bleed. Won't you come
Over and see me?

EVERY TIME I SEE

Every time I see your face, mind turns to mush
The feelings of wanting you and needing your touch
All but rush
with a flood that makes me need a crutch.
    Seeing your eyes I hope they won't tell me lies,
    Come close to me, so I can finally see.
    Can't wait to hear your voice, it is as love
Is the only choice.

ANOTHER DAY

Another day another lost
      What did it cost? Finding my way
        Through the dark, all my cries seem to
      Fall off the mark. Crying and Crying
    Yet no one to hear, left alone
      To dissolve in fear.

NEVER FELT THIS

Never felt this way before, never has
    My heart felt like it was going to soar.
        Thinking of you makes me want you more
           Needing your touch and feeling you
      Would be the best
Feeling in the world.

NEVER GONE SO

Never gone so far in life
        Never had I been so much
    In strife, reluctant to admit I'm at fault for
    The feelings that are
        Tearing me apart.

ANOTHER LONELY DAY

Another lonely day another night
    Without you, without your touch, with
  Out your smile, above all the miles
 Without you will cause me to fall deep
  Into depression, not to mention
The lesson learned from loving you
  Causing pain to be apart,
   Seeing your face would be all that I want.
So another day goes by and another moment
   Is surely lost.

DISTANCE

Never mind the distance,
 You are in my heart and soul
 Can't wait to see you again
 Long hours and days that
 I wait until the time comes
 Need to see your face.
 Can't not stand the silence
In my head, of not hearing
 Your voice and feeling your breath
 Can't wait to see you again,
I will hope to see you around the bend.

BEST OF MY DAYS

Best of my days, came and went
Best of my days never to see again
Before I went, I knew I was never
Going to see them again
They were the best of my days
Long days seem to be the best
Of my days, turned a corner
And they were all GONE
Can't change the past, cast change
The days, they went by so fast
They were the best of my days.
Now they are gone, all gone.

LOVE POEM FOR CRUSH

Want to tell you this for a long time
    That I look at your face and think you're so fine.
If you were to look at me and see how you make
    Me feel, that would be the best, so please
        Be my guest and talk to me.
      Staring at you makes my heart melt
    The touch of your skin would be
      What a dream I felt.
        To be with you would be a dream
  Come true, and
    Would cure me of being blue
Never have I felt this way
  It is a first for my days.
    Hope you will smile at me and make
Me feel alive, please notice me
    And see what you and I could be

SO MUCH TO SAY

So much to say, so little time
Miss the talks of moments of just you
And me, want to be so close to feel your soul
Want to talk for hours,
I would never run out of things
To say, so Much on my Mind,
will you ever hear it all?
MOMENTS run out as so does our time together
Heart breaks when I see the images in my head
Good and bad, only thing that keeps me alive
Inside as time runs out, so much to say
Yet not enough time.
I see your face and feel your
Presence here although will I ever
See you face to face
No time to say farewell
Although I will always think of you
And me as time goes by, with
Little time left
Our time was short but sweet
As the images crowd my mind like
A summer heat.

NEED TO SEE YOUR FACE

Need to see your face, need to feel your skin
Can't wait any longer, no matter how wrong it may be
Need to have you close to me, need you right now
Will you please come be with me?
Will you come and make me feel alive?
I want you so bad, I want to get away from the lies
Thinking of you melts my heart,
Being with you wants me to never part.
Do you feel the same, do you want to
Be with me until the end?

MOMENTS

So much to say so little time
        Miss the talks of just you and me
        Want to be so close, to feel your soul
        Want to talk for hours on end and never
    Run out of things to say, so much on my mind
        With you ever hear it?
    So much on my mind will you hear it all?
    MOMENTS run out so does our time together
Heart breaks when I see images of you
and I in my head.
    Good and bad the only thing that keeps me alive.
    SO much to say so little time, I see your face
and I hear
        your presence.
Although will I ever see your face again?
No time to say farewell, although I will always think
        Of you and me, with little time left.
        Our time was short but sweet as the
        Images crowd my mind like the summer heat.

YOU

Your dark hair is like a night sky
        blinding me with such beauty that can
not be ignored, the love i have for you
        shall be in my heart and stored.
        your face among the best i have seen
so attractive and so keen.

ALONE WITHOUT YOU

Not a day goes by where I don't miss you
Thinking of the days ahead without makes
me want to scream. It seems the dream is over
   Never will I see your face, never will I hear your
Voice, that revolves around my days.

EMERGED

It emerged as a sign, just slightly
        Yet it grew ever more as time
          Passed by, never to meet the eye
          Never to be full lies,
        Cannot let go cannot be set aside
Letting it go must be so it will not hide.

HEARTBREAK

Knowing that I can never have you
Makes my heart break apart
Nothing will ever be the same
And the shame will be with me
For as long as I live.

TIME OF DAY

Seeing your face, seeing that look
    Like no other one can, can change
       My life, **you're** such a bright light
      Never to fade, never to leave
   You above all make me believe

OPEN UP

    The way you open up to me
    The way you talk to me makes
        Me feel so alive, being without
        You I think I would die.
    Love how you speak your voice so
        Clear as anything I can seek.

COLDNESS

With the wind blowing harder and harder
Coldness spreads through my body
Piercing my skin, making me cringe
Knowing that the feeling will fade
Only thing that keeps me breathing

TELLING YOU HOW

To tell you how I feel would mean
        Opening up to someone who I care about
      In my heart there is no one but you
    That is without a doubt.
Loving you and knowing you are my goals
  I am hoping that I can be with you
    With my heart and soul.

WHERE I WANT TO BE

Where I want to be, your arms around me
    Nothing between us, seems like a dream
    You and me, alone, the world turned off
No sound but a slight switch of the light.

MOMENT OF MEETING

From the time I met you,
My feelings have turned true
Never have I felt this way before
Being with you makes my heart
Beat to the core
No one can take your place

EVERY TIME YOU

Every time I see you go, my heart breaks one
    By one, never to be the same until we meet
        Again, this shame will never end.
        The feeling of despair washes up upon me
        Until I get to see your face which frees me,
        From this cage.

EXCITED

So excited to see your face, to see that
      Smile of yours that light up my day
        The wait seems so long it
   Feels so wrong, need your touch, need it now
      Need it more than ever before.

FOR THE DAY

Can't wait for the day to see your face
    Your love is something I can't ever replace
   Need it more than life itself, to breathe you in
   To feel whole, to feel like I am one with you,
  Please give me a clue that you feel that way to

SUNNY DAY'S

Sunny day's sunny highs make me
    Feel so alive; wish it could be this bright
      All the time, never a cloud in the sky
      What a dream come true that would be,
    To see each and every day.

IN THE END

In the End
    Is this the end, or I am I just reaching
        My peak, all that I want and seek,
    Never to be within my reach.

www.ingramcontent.com/pod-product-compliance
Lightning Source LLC
Chambersburg PA
CBHW050047080526
44586CB00014B/1497